LIONS LEAVING:
COUNTING FROM 10 TO 1

by Amanda Doering Tourville

illustrated by Sharon Holm

Content Consultants: Paula J. Maida, PhD, and Terry Sinko, Instructional Support Teacher

magic
wagon

VISIT US AT
WWW.ABDOPUBLISHING.COM

Published by Magic Wagon, a division of the ABDO Publishing Group, 8000 West 78th Street, Edina, Minnesota 55439. Copyright © 2009 by Abdo Consulting Group, Inc. International copyrights reserved in all countries. All rights reserved. No part of this book may be reproduced in any form without written permission from the publisher.

Looking Glass Library™ is a trademark and logo of Magic Wagon.

Printed in the United States.

Text by Amanda Doering Tourville
Illustrations by Sharon Holm
Edited by Patricia Stockland
Interior layout and design by Becky Daum
Cover design by Becky Daum

Library of Congress Cataloging-in-Publication Data

Tourville, Amanda Doering, 1980–
   Lions leaving : counting from 10 to 1 / by Amanda Doering Tourville ; illustrated by Sharon Holm.
      p. cm. — (Count the critters)
   ISBN 978-1-60270-264-6
   1. Counting—Juvenile literature. 2. Lions—Juvenile literature. I. Holm, Sharon Lane, ill. II. Title.
   QA113.T686 2009
   513.2'11—dc22
                          2008001627

Counting backward is as much fun as counting forward! Count backward as the lions leave the watering hole.

Ten lions drink water from a
watering hole.

One lion is tired. It flops down under a tree to nap. Ten take away one is nine.

Nine lions are left to drink water from a watering hole. A crocodile snaps its jaws, scaring one lion away. Nine take away one is eight.

4 3 2 1 9 – 1 = **8**

Eight lions remain to drink water from a watering hole. The sun is getting hot. One lion leaves to look for shade. Eight take away one is seven.

4 3 2 1 8 – 1 = 7

Seven lions are left to drink water from a watering hole. One lion's cub wanders away. The lion trots after it.

Seven take away one is six.

4   3   2   1   7−1=**6**

Six lions remain to drink water from a watering hole. One lion is hungry. It chases a gazelle across the plain. Six take away one is five.

Five lions are left to drink water from a watering hole. One lion scampers away to find its friend. Five take away one is four.

Four lions remain to drink water from a watering hole. One lion walks away to groom its paws. Four take away one is three.

Three lions are left to drink water from a watering hole. It is time for a bath.

One lion steps aside to lick its cub
clean. Three take away one is two.

Two lions remain to drink water from a watering hole. One lion has an itch on his back. It rolls away in the dirt. Two take away one is one.

One lonely lion is left to drink water from a watering hole. Ten, nine, eight, seven, six, five, four, three, two, one thirsty lion. Whew!

words to Know

groom — to clean and make a neat appearance.

plain — a flat or rolling stretch of land without trees.

scamper — to move quickly.

shade — an outdoor area that sun cannot reach.

trot — to move at a speed between a walk and a run.

watering hole — a pool of water where animals come to drink.

web Sites

To learn more about counting from 10 to 1, visit ABDO Publishing Company on the World Wide Web at **www.abdopublishing.com**. Web sites about counting are featured on our Book Links page. These links are routinely monitored and updated to provide the most current information available.